THE WISDOM
of the
ENGLISH MYSTICS

Robert Way

THE WISDOM OF THE ENGLISH MYSTICS

THE AUTHOR

Robert Way is an antiquarian bookseller in New-market. He is married, with five children and four grandchildren. After reading for a degree in classics and rural economy at Cambridge he spent a long period farming and breeding thoroughbred horses, before taking up bookselling. He has now handed the business over to his son in order that he may devote himself to travelling widely in search of books.

Other Books in The Wisdom Series

THE WISDOM OF THE EARLY BUDDHISTS
Geoffrey Parrinder

THE WISDOM OF THE DESERT
Thomas Merton

THE WISDOM OF THE ANCIENT EGYPTIANS
William MacQuitty

THE WISDOM OF THE FOREST
Geoffrey Parrinder

THE WISDOM OF THE JEWISH MYSTICS
Alan Unterman

THE WISDOM OF THE SPANISH MYSTICS
Stephen Clissold

THE WISDOM OF THE SUFIS
Kenneth Cragg

THE WISDOM OF THE ZEN MASTERS
Irmgard Schloegl

Published by
New Directions

THE WISDOM OF
THE ENGLISH MYSTICS

COMPILED BY
ROBERT WAY

A NEW DIRECTIONS BOOK

7904302

Thanks are due for permission to quote from the following sources: for lines from "Safety," in *The Collected Poems of Rupert Brooke*, reprinted by permission of Dodd, Mead & Company; for excerpts from "East Coker" (*Four Quartets*) in *Collected Poems* by T. S. Eliot (Copyright 1936 by Harcourt Brace Jovanovich, Inc.; Copyright © 1963, 1964 by T. S. Eliot), reprinted by permission of Harcourt Brace Jovanovich, Inc.; for lines from "The Ballad of Sir Bors," in *Poems* by John Masefield (Copyright 1912 by Macmillan Publishing Co., Inc.; renewed 1940 by John Masefield), reprinted by permission of Macmillan Publishing Co., Inc.; for passages from *An Anthology of the Love of God* by Evelyn Underhill, reprinted by permission of A. R. Mowbray & Co., Ltd.

Manufactured in the United States of America
First published as New Directions Paperbook 466 in 1978 by arrangement with Sheldon Press, London

Library of Congress Cataloging in Publication Data

Main entry under title:
The Wisdom of the English mystics.
    (A New Directions Book)
    (Wisdom series)
    1. Mysticism—England—Quotations, maxims, etc.
I. Way, Robert.   II. Series: Wisdom series
(New York)
BV5085.W59 1978   248'.22'0941   78-6435
ISBN 0-8112-0700-5

New Directions Books are published for James Laughlin
by New Directions Publishing Corporation,
333 Sixth Avenue, New York 10014

TABLE OF CONTENTS

THE WISDOM OF
THE ENGLISH MYSTICS

*

STORIES AND SAYINGS

THE WISDOM OF
THE ENGLISH MYSTICS

WHEN writing of the mystics it is essential first to make clear what one means by this term. The word mystic which originally referred to those initiated in the ancient Greek mystery religions came to refer specifically to certain seekers after God who sought him in a particular way, a way which I will try to elucidate. Unfortunately, in modern times the word has come to be used very loosely and is applied to almost anyone having or claiming to have powers outside ordinary human experience: visionaries, spiritualists and even magicians.

The doctrine of the true mystic is essentially summed up in the Epistle of St John. 'Love is of God and everyone who loves is born of God and knows God, but he who does not love does not know God for God is love.' This love must be purged of all self interest. We must love God for Himself alone and not for any good gifts he may give us, or else we love God's gifts and not God himself. All other things we must love for his sake. It is true that to a very few favoured souls God does give extraordinary benefits even, in a very few cases, the beatific vision and enables them to see, as Dante says (in Chesterton's translation), 'the unfathomable ray of rays which of itself and by itself is true'. But this is an exceptional favour neither to be expected nor sought for. The true mystic echoes rather the words of St Francis Xavier:

My God I love thee not because
I hope for Heaven thereby,
Or because they that love thee not
Must burn eternally.
Not with the hope of gaining aught,
Not seeking a reward,
But as thyself hath lovéd me
O ever Loving Lord.

Indeed we find generally that the true mystics suffer long periods of dereliction when it seems that God has hidden himself from them and also they very often feel physical pain or worldly distress, yet this does not undermine their love for and trust in God.

Despite the many different ways in which the mystic writers have expressed their striving after union with God, there is only one true mystical way. The reason for the variations is explained by Father Augustine Baker in his commentary on *The Cloud of Unknowing*.

The truth is, that all mystic writers in expressing the spiritual course that they have run, seem to differ wholly from one another, whereas the difference is in words and terms not in content. The reason for their seeming difference is that spiritual matters can only with difficulty, if at all, be expressed in meaningful words since there are no proper words which serve for this purpose. But the mystics, anxious to express themselves as best they can, use such terms as they think will express their meaning, each one in his own way.

In spite of the variety of expression, the essentials of the mystic way can be fairly easily defined. The first essential for those who would seek God is humility. Without this the road is exceedingly dangerous, and those without humility can easily be deluded by the powers of evil, hence the repeated warnings against pride given by the mystical writers. The author of *The Cloud*, especially, gives the warning, 'For I tell you truly that the devil has his contemplatives as God has his.'

Some mystics have had physical manifestations: voices, burning sensations and ocular visions, but these have always been regarded by the Church and mystical teachers with grave suspicion and were very carefully examined before being accepted as coming from God.

The advance to God is made in a divine darkness which the author of *The Cloud* calls a cloud of unknowing. God is so far above all human conception that the only way in which he can be comprehended is through love and desire, since knowledge and the senses can in no way reach him.

The idea of this divine darkness originates with Dionysius the Areopagite and is most clearly stated in his letter to Dorotheus the Deacon:

The divine darkness is the inaccessible light in which God dwells and since he is invisible by reason of the overwhelming brightness, and inaccessible through the supernatural excess of light, it follows that whoever deserves to know and see God by the very fact that he neither sees or knows him attains to that which is above all sight and knowledge, and at the same time comes to know that God is beyond all perception and understanding.

Although it has not been conclusively proved that the Dionysius the Areopagite who wrote these works was not the man mentioned in the Acts of the Apostles (17.34), it is generally accepted that he was a fourth-century monk who adopted the name to give his words greater authority. His influence on mystical thought is incalculable. Indeed the author of *The Cloud* translated one of his works *Denoise Hid Divinite*.

There was one problem which greatly troubled many mystics. If God is all loving and all powerful why does he allow anyone to suffer eternal damnation without hope of redemption and why does he allow sin in the world? Some teachers seem to think that contemplating the torments of the damned is part of the reward of the blessed, but this is certainly not the view of the true mystic for whom another's good is more important than his own. Margery Kempe refused to believe in eternal damnation and suffered great torment until she changed her mind. William Law in later life believed in the ultimate overcoming of evil and salvation for all. And to Julian of Norwich was revealed as a divine mystery full of hope: 'Sin is necessary but all shall be well, all shall be well, all shall be very well'.

It may be asked what relevance the works of the mystics have today Their teaching is in fact very relevant in the present context. All over the country one finds the most unexpected people—particularly young people—searching for God. Often they follow strange, esoteric doctrines belonging to religions of cultures other than their own, such as little known Zen Buddhist or Hindu sects, while if they but knew it, their own religion affords a way to find God founded on their own cultural heritage.

It may further be objected that the mystics' search for God is merely selfish and does no good for the world. It is true that when mystics have been in positions of authority they have nearly always been overthrown and their work corrupted and undone by the orthodox powers of the world. Nonetheless the imputation is untrue; for mysticism is like a light which, although it does not move or work visibly, illumines all around it, so that these often obscure lovers of God lighten the darkness of the world. They are like a little leaven bringing life to a Church which would otherwise be heavy and inert.

The earliest English mystical writer of importance was Aelred, Abbot of Rievaulx (1100–67). He had been steward to the royal household of King David of Scotland until he visited the Abbey of Rievaulx when on business in Yorkshire. He was so impressed that, despite great inner conflict, he decided to remain there. Later, when on Abbey business in Rome, he became acquainted with St Bernard whose teaching deeply influenced him. He subsequently became Abbot of Rievaulx. His most important works were *The Mirror of Charity* and *Christian Friendship*. Of his stature as a mystical writer there can be no doubt but he somehow stands outside the main stream of English mystical tradition, partly because he wrote in Latin and partly because of his classical education.

In 1237 a cleric, believed to be Richard Poor, Bishop of Salisbury, wrote the Ancrene (or Anchoresses) Rule for three sisters who had a cell attached to the church at Tarrant Keynston in Dorset. Although this might not really be considered by some as a mystical work, nonetheless it was a very important introduction to the English mystical tradition.

Fourteenth-century England was in a state of misery and ferment. The black death swept the country, killing a third of the population; land became derelict and the surviving rural population was oppressed and discontented, depleted by the constant demand for men to fight in the French wars. This discontent led later to Wat Tyler's rebellion in 1381. Then, too, the authority of the Church was beginning to be undermined by Wyclif's followers, the Lollards, who claimed the right to personal interpretation of Scripture. And the Papacy which had been a stabilizing influence for centuries was greatly discredited by the abdication and imprisonment of the saintly Coelestine and the assumption of power by the legalist Benedict and the French-dominated popes of Avignon. It was this troubled century that produced the greatest number of important English mystics. The earliest of the fourteenth-century mystical writers was Richard Rolle who was born in about 1300 at Thornton-le-Dale in Yorkshire. He went up to Oxford under the sponsorship of Thomas Neville, Archdeacon of Durham, but left without a degree at the age of nineteen. Almost immediately he left home and became a hermit living in various places, eventually becoming spiritual director to a small community of nuns at Hampole near Doncaster. Many details of his life are preserved in the *Legenda*, or edifying lessons, which are included in the mass prepared by the nuns of

Hampole in expectation of his canonization. This, however, never took place. Richard Rolle wrote a large number of prose and verse works both in English and in Latin. His writings show a less gentle spirit than do those of most of the later mystics but resound with a great joy in God. In his mystical state he felt a sensation of burning and heard heavenly music. His preoccupation with these physical manifestations was a dangerous precedent to his less balanced followers and was partly responsible for the serious warnings about manifestations of this kind by later writers, especially the author of *The Cloud of Unknowing*.

The Cloud of Unknowing is, perhaps, the most important mystical work in the English language. Although nothing at all is known about its author, his works can be dated to the middle of the fourteenth century and it has been conjectured that he came from the eastern counties. He wrote six other minor treatises and his influence on subsequent mystical thought was immense. Another important mystical writer was Walter Hilton who was Canon of Thurgarton in Northamptonshire. Nothing else is known of his life. His best known work was *The Scale of Perfection* which was probably the most widely read of all the mystical works of that period. It circulated in numerous manuscripts and was printed as early as 1494. From it Father Augustine Baker precised *The Advice to a Pilgrim* which is perhaps the most complete short guide to the spiritual life there is. Another very important work of Hilton's for the present age is *The Mixed Life*, which shows how a spiritual and active life can be combined. The other two mystical writers

9

of the period were both women. Julian was an anchoress or female hermit attached to the Church of St Julian at Norwich. Her work is based on a series of visions which she had when very ill in 1373 and her meditations on them during the following twenty years. Nothing was known of her apart from what could be gathered from her own book, until the book of Margery Kempe was discovered. This contains an interesting account of an interview which Margery had with her.

In 1501 Wynkyn de Worde published a small book of extracts from the work of Margery Kempe which was reprinted by Henry Pipwell in 1521. Nothing else was known about her until in 1934 Miss A. E. Allen identified a manuscript in the library of Colonel W. Butler Bowden as the Book of Margery Kempe and a very intriguing book it proved to be. Margery Kempe was the daughter of John Brunham, several times the Mayor of Kings Lynn, and in 1393 she married John Kempe of Lynn. Shortly after this she began to brood on a sin she could not bring herself to confess. So obsessed was she with her sin that she became deranged and had to be bound night and day, until she had a vision of Christ who cured her. However, this left her overendowed with the gift of tears and the sight of the Host or a mention of the Passion made her burst out sighing and sobbing which, not surprisingly, many priests found so distracting that they forbade her to attend their services. The book tells of her travels and adventures on pilgrimages to Jerusalem, of her visit to St James Compostella and of a journey to Germany; also of her questioning before high ecclesiastical authorities on suspicion of Lollardy from which she emerged vindicated. In fact, it is noticeable that she generally fared better with the higher authorities of the Church than with the lower and with foreigners than with her own countrymen. Whatever her faults there is no doubting her supreme trust in God and her humility of spirit which sometimes made her distrust the source of her revelation. She was utterly fearless and very grateful to those who were kind to her. She seems to have been widely known and the cause of much controversy. She had a very vivid imagination and seemed actually to see the incidents of our Lord's life. One story in particular which she told against herself although she denied its truth, is worth recalling here. It was said that one day when she was out to dinner some red herring—a coarse, unpopular fish—and pike, which was considered a great delicacy, were served. Whereupon she exclaimed, 'Ah thou false flesh you would now eat red herring but you shall not have your will' and then tucked into the pike.

It is noticeable that with the exception of Margery Kempe, little is known of these mystical writers. They were men and women of interior life who sought to perfect themselves and not to try to change the course of events except by their example and writing.

One cannot understand the religious climate of this period without taking into account the phenomenon of the anchoress. These were women, often of good family, who lived in cells attached to certain churches. We are able to get a very good idea of their lives from the *Ancrene Riwle*. Once they were installed in these cells they never left them but devoted themselves to

11

prayer and contemplation. But their lives were not uncomfortable, their cells consisted of two or three rooms and there might be a walled garden. They had servants to look after them and run messages for them and they could talk to people through their windows. They sometimes acted as spiritual advisers as was the case with Julian, but they were generally dependent for their sustenance on the charity of a patron.

The less pleasant aspect of an anchoress's life is also told in the *Ancrene Riwle*. 'Always to be held of no account, to beg one's livelihood if need be like a vagabond and to be another's pensioner as you are, my dear sisters, and often to suffer the arrogance of those who might once have been your thralls.'

Anchoresses were fairly numerous. Their influence on mystical literature cannot be over-emphasized. Not only do we have the *Ancrene Riwle* but Julian herself was an anchoress and two of Richard Rolle's works were written for the anchoress Margaret Kirkeby. Hilton's *Scale of Perfection* is addressed to his ghostly Sister in Jesus Christ who, from his remarks about the enclosing of her body, would appear to have been an anchoress. Margery Kempe is described as an anchoress in Henry Pipwell's edition of her work. She may perhaps have become one in later life but it is more probable that it is an error of the editor's who considered that no one but an anchoress would have written a work of this type. There were also men who lived as hermits but they were not under the strict rules which anchoresses had to observe nor were they bound to one place. Richard Rolle was a hermit and some blamed him for the way he moved from one place to another.

I myself think that the author of *The Cloud* was a hermit for if, as some conjecture, he was a country parson or monk, it is difficult to understand his strong reactions to those who said that a man should only take up the contemplative life if he had prior provision for his maintenance. He also seems to speak from personal experience when he insists that God will provide what is needed or give the strength to do without.

The next flowering of the mystic spirit was in the seventeenth century when England was once again torn by discontent and civil strife and the Church, Protestant now, torn apart by internal dissensions. On the Catholic side there was Father Augustine Baker who was born of Protestant parents at Abergavenny in 1575. He went to Pembroke College, Oxford, and was later converted to Catholicism by what he considered a miraculous escape from death. He was riding along, presumably deep in contemplation, when his horse suddenly stopped and he found himself in the middle of a narrow bridge which got narrower and narrower the further it continued. There was no room to turn the horse round and there was a deep drop into a gorge on either side. He despaired of his life, shut his eyes and prayed fervently. The next thing he knew, the horse was facing the way he had come, he did not know how, and he could only attribute it to the miraculous intervention of God. Those who know the perverted sense of humour and lively sense of self preservation of the Welsh breed of horse may be forgiven for doubting the supernatural element in this,

13

nonetheless the horse converted him just as effectively as if it had spoken like Balaam's ass.

Father Augustine became a Benedictine monk and was ordained a priest in 1619. After serving as chaplain to a community of nuns at Cambray for whom he wrote most of his works, he was sent on a mission to England. His death, probably from the plague, in 1641 just forestalled his martyrdom. In 1659 Father Serenus Cressy wrote an account of his life and also collected and edited his works under the title *Holy Wisdom*. This book is the fullest and most systematic account of the mystic way written in English, but it is very long and rather difficult to read.

On the Protestant side there was George Herbert who was born near Montgomery in 1593 and after making his name as Orator at Oxford University became an ideal parish priest at Bemerton near Salisbury and a mystical poet. There was also the poet Henry Vaughan known as the Silurist and the Swan of Usk. He was born at Newton near Skethrock on Usk in 1622, educated at Jesus College, Oxford and became a doctor in his native town where he died in 1695.

But the most important of all was Thomas Traherne, son of a Herefordshire shoemaker, born in 1637. He took his degree at Brasenose College, Oxford, and became rector of Credenhill in Herefordshire and Chaplain to Sir Orlando Bridgeman, Keeper of the Great Seal. He died in 1674. His poems were not published until 1906 and *Centuries*, his most important work, until 1908. It is indeed fortunate that the manuscripts had not perished in the interval.

During the seventeenth century there was also an

14

outburst of mystical experience and writing outside the established Churches. Most notable was George Fox the Quaker as we can see from his journal, and the Cambridge Platonists, the most important of whom was John Smith. Among the Philadelphians, too, Jane Leade amid her strange apocalyptic writings shows an occasional gleam of true mystical experience.

The eighteenth century produced only one outstanding mystic, William Law who, when he lost his university appointment through being a non-juror and refusing to swear allegiance to William III, became tutor to the father of Edward Gibbon the historian. He was much influenced by the strange doctrines of the German mystic Jacob Boeme, but was nonetheless a courageous and original thinker.

William Blake is the only outstanding figure of Georgian times and from the point of view of mysticism he is a controversial figure for he is in reality more a visionary than mystic and furthermore his inspiration is really more visual than intellectual. Evelyn Underhill says (*Mysticism*, Appendix), 'So individual was his vision, so strange the elements from which his symbolic reconstructions were built up, that he failed in the attempt to convey it to other men.' He had, however, an almost Franciscan sympathy for living creatures.

It is difficult to write about modern mystics. There are so few mystical writers, or perhaps one should say, so many, but of insufficient stature, that it is hard to decide who to include and who to leave out. The one outstanding figure is Evelyn Underhill (1875–1941), who is prominent both as a poet and as a prose writer.

Many people have had some mystical experience but

15

lack the power to express it. But we find in the poets who have the gift of expression, accounts of mystical experience, sometimes rather unexpected such as those in Lord Tennyson's 'The Ancient Sage' and in Wordsworth's passage in the 'Intimations of Immortality'. The latter closely corresponds with the work of Thomas Traherne, which he could not possibly have read.

Possibly the most interesting of all are the so-called nature mystics. Richard Jefferies, author of *The Story of My Heart*, had real and prolonged mystical experiences but his refusal to believe in God led him to write: 'I prayed that I might touch to the unalterable existence infinitely higher than deity'. He did not seem to realize or accept that such a higher existence was, in fact, God and indeed that Dionysius in his letter to Caius described God as higher than deity.

An anthology of this kind is bound to be coloured by the beliefs and predilections of the compiler. Someone else using the same material would probably have produced a very different book. While the essentials would, of necessity, be the same, the emphasis would be different, probably with much more on contemplative prayer which I have never found useful.

Further I must warn the reader that in many instances, for the sake of brevity, some sentences have been omitted without this being indicated; also archaisms have been rendered into modern usage.

STORIES AND SAYINGS

★ I ★

WILLIAM BLAKE wrote in his letters: The tree which moves some to tears of joy is in the eyes of others only a green thing that stands in the way.

★ II ★

WILLIAM BLAKE wrote in *Jerusalem*:

I rest not upon my great task
To open the Eternal Worlds, to open the immortal
  Eyes
Of man towards the World of Thought: into Eternity
Ever expanding in the Bosom of God, the Human
  Imagination.
O Saviour, pour upon me thy Spirit of meekness and
  love,
Annihilate the Selfhood in me: be thou all my life.

★ III ★

EVELYN UNDERHILL tells of God:

I come in little things,
Saith the Lord:
Yea! on the glancing wings
Of eager birds, the softly pattering feet
Of furred and gentle beasts, I come to meet
Your hard and wayward heart. In brown bright eyes
That peep from out of the brake, I stand confest.
On every nest

Where feathery Patience is content to brood
And leaves her pleasures for the high emprize
Of motherhood—
There doth My Godhead rest.

★ IV ★

RICHARD ROLLE said: Let us make God the beginning
and end of our love, for he is the fountain from which
all good things flow and into him alone they flow
back. Let him therefore be the beginning of our love,
he whom we love for himself alone and let him be the
end through whom we love whatever ought to be
loved, and to whom we refer everything which we
love and by which we are loved. This indeed shows
the perfection of love, that the whole intention of the
mind and the whole hidden operation of the heart is
directed upwards into divine love to such an extent
that the force of pure love and joy of holy affection are
so overwhelming that worldly delight and the pleasures
of the flesh would not please us even if they were
allowed. And that although there were no torments
for sinners in hell nor might any reward be expected
for the good in heaven we would be no more willing
on this account to cast ourselves off from the Beloved.

★ V ★

LOVE is the true price of love.

★ VI ★

AELRED OF RIEVAULX wrote: I think you must know
that when first God comes to you, he sometimes mixes

18

the sweetness of the pleasure with fear. The second time also he often uses a goad of fear mixed with pleasure but the essence of the first is fear, of the second the sweetness of consolation. The third time perfect love casts out fear. The beginning of wisdom is the fear of the Lord, but the perfection of wisdom is the love of the Lord. The beginning is in fear, the perfection in delight. The first two are the labour, the last the reward.

★ VII ★

THOMAS TRAHERNE gives an extraordinarily vivid account of his early infancy: The pure and unsullied perception I had from the womb and that divine light with which I was born are to this day the best in which I can see the universe. By the gift of God they attended me into the world and by his especial favour I remember them still. Everything appeared new and strange at first, inexpressibly rare, delightful and beautiful. I was a little stranger who at my entrance into the world was saluted and surrounded by innumerable joys. My knowledge was divine. I knew by intuition those things which since I have had to collect again by the highest reason. My very ignorance was advantageous. All things were spotless, pure and glorious, yes, and infinitely mine and joyful and precious. I did not know there were any sins or complaints or laws. I did not dream of poverty, strife or vices. All tears and quarrels were hidden from my eyes. Heaven and earth sang my Creator's praises. All time was eternity. The corn was radiant and immortal wheat which would never be reaped nor was ever sown, I thought it had stood everlastingly. The dust and stones of the street were as precious as gold. The gates were at first the end of the world. The green trees, when I saw them first through one of the gates, transported and ravished me. Their sweetness and unusual beauty made my heart leap. Men were like angels. Boys and girls tumbling in the street and playing were moving jewels. I did not know that they had been born or must die. The city seemed to stand in Eden or to be built in heaven; everything in it was mine. The skies, too, were mine and so were the sun and moon and stars. The whole world was mine and I alone looked at and enjoyed it. But with much trouble I was corrupted and made to learn the dirty devices of the world which I am now unlearning and becoming as it were a little child again, so that I may enter into the Kingdom of God.

⋆ VIII ⋆

WILLIAM WORDSWORTH the poet wrote:

> Our birth is but a sleep and a forgetting:
> The Soul that rises with us, our life's Star,
> Hath had elsewhere its setting,
> And cometh from afar:
> Not in entire forgetfulness,
> And not in utter nakedness,
> But trailing clouds of glory do we come
> From God, who is our home:
> Heaven lies round us in our infancy!
> Shades of the prison-house begin to close
> Upon the growing boy,
> But he beholds the light, and whence it flows,

He sees it in his joy;
The youth, who daily further from the east
Must travel, still is Nature's priest,
And by the vision splendid
Is on his way attended;
At length the man perceives it die away
And fade into the light of common day.

* IX *

THOMAS TRAHERNE tells us how his early understanding was destroyed: The light that shone in my
infancy in its original and innocent clarity was totally
eclipsed; so that I had to learn it all again. If you ask
me how it was eclipsed, indeed by the customs and
manners of men which like contrary winds blew it
out: by an innumerable company of other common
and worthless things which like so many loads of earth
and dung overwhelmed and buried it: by the im-
petuous torrent of wrong desires in all others whom I
saw and knew, that carried me away and alienated me
from it: by a whole sea of other matters and concerns
that covered and drowned it: finally by the evil
influence of a bad education that did not foster and
cherish it. All men's thoughts and words were about
other matters. They all prized new things of which I
did not dream. I was a stranger and unacquainted with
them. I was little and reverenced their authority. I was
weak and easily guided by their example, ambitious
too and wishing to win their approval. Not finding
a single syllable in anyone's mouth about these things,
by degrees they vanished and at last these heavenly

21

great and stable treasures to which I was born were as wholly forgotten as if they had never been. If anyone had spoken of it, it would have been the easiest thing in the world to have taught me and made me believe that heaven and earth were God's house and that he gave it to me: that earth was better than gold and that water, every drop of it a precious jewel; that these were great and living treasures and all other riches were dross in comparison.

⋆ X ⋆

WILLIAM WORDSWORTH also speaks of the fading of his early knowledge:

There was a time when meadow, grove, and stream,
The earth, and every common sight,
To me did seem
Apparelled in celestial light,
The glory and the freshness of a dream.
It is not now as it has been of yore;—
Turn wheresoe'er I may,
By night or day,
The things which I have seen I now can see no more.

⋆ XI ⋆

EVELYN UNDERHILL wrote: More and more as we go on with the Christian life we learn the absolute power of the Spirit over circumstance. God in his richness and freedom coming as a factor into every situation; overruling the stream of events which make up our earthly existence and through these events moulding our souls, quickening and modifying our lives at every point. The more freely, simply and humbly the soul is abandoned to this penetrating and encompassing power, the more it becomes conscious—dimly yet surely—of its constant, stern, yet loving action through all the circumstances of life.

★ XII ★

THOMAS TRAHERNE said: Think of a river, a drop of water, an apple or a grain of sand, an ear of corn or a herb. God knows the infinite excellencies of each better than we do. He sees how it relates to angels and men. How it proceeds from the most perfect Lover to the most perfectly beloved. How it represents all his attributes. How it leads by the best of means to the best of ends. For this reason it cannot be loved too much. God the author and God the end is to be loved in it. Angels and men are to be loved in it and it must be esteemed highly for all their sakes. O what a treasure is in every grain of sand when truly understood! Who can love anything that God made too much? His infinite goodness and wisdom and power and glory are in it. What would a world be if everything were loved as it ought to be!

★ XIII ★

GEORGE FOX wrote in his journal: Now was I come up in spirit through the flaming sword into the paradise of God. All things were new, and all the creation gave another smell unto me than before, beyond what words can utter. I knew nothing but pureness and

23

innocency and righteousness, being renewed up into the image of God by Christ Jesus, so that I was come up to the state of Adam which he was in before he fell.

★ XIV ★

GEORGE FOX wrote in his journal: One time, I was under very great suffering in my spirit and under the very sense of death; but when I came out of it, standing in the will of God, a heavenly breathing arose in my soul to the Lord. Then did I see the heavens opened and the glory of God shined over all.

★ XV ★

JANE LEADE wrote: As I was considering the high and weighty work to which we were called, my spirit was immediately caught up into a high region that was all calm and still, where I saw no figures or images, but there was a wonderful light which flowed into me like a river. Then it was opened to me that this was the creating light from which all being did proceed and that what was now expected as a new creation must be brought forth from the stillness of the light.

★ XVI ★

RICHARD JEFFERIES tells in *The Story of My Heart*: Having drunk deeply of heaven above and felt the most glorious beauty of the day, and remembering the old, old sea, which (as it seemed to me) was but just yonder at the edge, I now become lost, and absorbed into the being or existence of the universe. I felt deep down into the earth under, and high above into the sky, further still to the sun and stars. Still further beyond the stars into the hollows of space and losing thus my separateness of being came to feel like a part of the whole.

⋆XVII⋆

LORD TENNYSON tells us that the following verse was an account of an experience of his own:

And more, my son! for more than once when I
Sat all alone, revolving in myself
The word that is the symbol of myself,
The mortal limit of the Self was loosed,
And passed in the Nameless, as a cloud
Melts into Heaven. I touch'd my limbs, the limbs
Were strange not mine—and yet no shade of doubt,
But utter clearness, thro' loss of Self
The gain of such large life as matched with ours
Were Sun to spark—unshadowable in words
Themselves but shadows of a shadow world.

⋆XVIII⋆

RICHARD JEFFERIES wrote: It was the tall firs which pleased me most; the glance rose up the flame shaped fir tree tapering to its green tip, and above was the pure azure sky. By the aid of the tree I felt the sky more. By the aid of everything beautiful I felt myself, and in that intense sense of consciousness prayed for greater perfection of the soul and body.

★ XIX ★

RICHARD JEFFERIES wrote: Touching the crumble of earth, the blade of grass, the thyme flower, breathing the earth-encircling air, thinking of the sea and the sky, holding out my hand for a sunbeam to touch it, prone on the sward in token of deep reverence, thus I prayed that I might touch to the unutterable existence infinitely higher than deity.

★ XX ★

JULIAN OF NORWICH wrote: God is all that is good, in my sight, and the goodness that everything has is he.

★ XXI ★

EVELYN UNDERHILL wrote: Men who thus acquiesce in life and offer her their full love and service, find their advances met halfway. All things become friendly to them because they have been adopted into the mighty family of the sons of God. In every living thing they discern the movement and self-expression of that Spirit which they serve. New kingdoms of life are disclosed to them! the uncreated light illumines for them the most painfully artistic villas and the meanest streets. They feel with that poignant emotion for which man has yet to find a name, the passionate vitality which burns in every blade of grass and budding spray. They perceive and worship, though they may not understand, the steady rhythm of growth by which they are surrounded, the perpetual unfolding of new beauty and new power: within themselves they feel the pulse of that same urgent Spirit and know themselves to be concerned in the stupendous adventure of the universe.

⋆ XXII ⋆

WILLIAM LAW says of God: He is the love itself, the unmixed, unmeasurable love, doing nothing but from love, giving nothing but gifts of love to everything that he has made; requiring nothing of all his creatures but the spirit and fruits of that love, which brought them into being. Oh, how sweet is this contemplation of the height and depth of the riches of divine love!

⋆ XXIII ⋆

HENRY VAUGHAN wrote the following poem called 'The Shower':

'Twas so; I saw thy birth. That drowsy lake
From her faint bosom breath'd thee, the disease
Of her sick waters and infectious ease.
    But now at even,
    Too gross for heaven,
Thou fall'st in tears and weep'st for thy mistake.

Ah! it is so with me; oft have I press'd
Heaven with lazy breath; but fruitless this
Pierced not; love only can with quick access
    Unlock the way,
    When all else stray,
The smoke and exhalations of the breast.

27

Yet, if as thou dost melt, and with thy train
Of drops make soft the Earth, my eyes could weep
O'er my hard heart, that's bound up and asleep;
   Perhaps at last,
   Some such showers past,
My God would give a sunshine after rain.

XXIV

WALTER HILTON wrote: Remember the might, the
wisdom and the goodness of our Lord in all his
creatures for in as much as we cannot see God fully in
himself while we live here, therefore we must behold
him, love him and dread him and wonder at his might
and his wisdom and his goodness in his works and in
his creatures.

XXV

EVELYN UNDERHILL used the following analogy:
Nothing in all nature is so lovely and so vigorous, so
perfectly at home in its environment, as a fish in the
sea. Its surroundings give to it a beauty, quality and
power which is not its own. We take it out, and at
once a poor dull limp thing, fit for nothing, is gasping
away its life. So the soul sunk in God, living the life of
prayer is supported, filled, transformed in beauty, by a
vitality and power which is not its own. The souls of
the saints are so powerful because they are utterly
immersed in the Spirit; their whole life is prayer.

XXVI

THOMAS TRAHERNE meditates: That violence wherewith sometimes a man dotes upon one creature, is but

a little spark of that love even towards all which lurks in his nature. We are made to love both to satisfy the necessity of our active nature, and to answer the beauties in every creature. By love our souls are married and soldered to the creatures: and it is our duty like God to be united to them all. We must love them infinitely but in God, and for God: and God in them: namely all His excellencies manifested in them. When we dote upon the perfections and beauties of some one creature: we do not love that too much, but other things too little. Never was anything in this world loved too much, but many things have been loved in a false way: and all in too short a measure.

* XXVII *

THOMAS TRAHERNE wrote: Think of an outstandingly beautiful woman. Some have seen the beauties of heaven in such a person. It is of no use saying they loved too much. I dare say there are ten thousand beauties in that creature which they have not seen. They loved her not too much but for the wrong reasons and not so much for wrong reasons as for little ones. They love a woman for sparkling eyes and curled hair, lily white breasts and ruddy cheeks whom they should love also for being God's image, queen of the universe, beloved by angels, redeemed by Jesus Christ, an heiress of heaven, a child of God. But these excellencies they do not know. Perhaps they love her but they do not love God more, nor mankind as much nor heaven and earth at all. So being defective in other things they perish from what seemed to be excess of

29

that. Confidentially I dare say that every person in the whole world ought to be loved as much as this; and she, if there is any reason for difference, more than she is. But God being loved infinitely more will be infinitely more our joy and our heart will be more with him. So that no man can be in danger of loving others too much who loves God as he ought.

★ XXVIII ★

THE PROVERB says: He that hunts two hares catches neither.

★ XXIX ★

WILLIAM BLAKE wrote:

> Kill not the moth or butterfly
> For the last judgement draweth nigh.

★ XXX ★

EVELYN UNDERHILL taught: We offer ourselves in one way or another, to try and work for God. We want, as it were, to be among the sheepdogs employed by the Good Shepherd. Have you ever watched a good sheepdog at work? He is not an emotional animal. He goes on with his job quite steadily, takes no notice of bad weather, rough ground or his own comfort. He seldom or never stops to be stroked. Yet his faithfulness and intimate communion with his master are one of the loveliest things in the world. Now and then he looks at the shepherd. And when the time comes for rest, they are generally to be found together. Let this be the model of your love.

✶XXXI✶

RICHARD ROLLE said: A human mind cannot feel the fire of eternal love unless first it abandons perfectly all the vanities of the world and at the same time sets out to study heavenly things and without ceasing to desire divine love and to love every creature in due measure. For if everything that we love, we love for God's sake, we rather love God in it than the thing itself and so we delight not in it but in God whom we shall enjoy in glory forever.

✶XXXII✶

HE LOSES nothing that loses not God.

✶XXXIII✶

THOMAS TRAHERNE wrote: What rule do you think I followed? Indeed a strange one but the best in the whole world. I was guided by an implicit faith in God's goodness, and therefore was led to the study of the most obvious and common things. For I thought God being, as we believe, infinite in goodness it must be in accordance with his nature that the best things should be the most common and only things that are worthless scarce. Then I began to enquire as to what things were most common; air, light, heaven and earth, water, sun, trees, men and women, cities, churches, etc., these I found common and open to all. Rubies, pearls,

diamonds, gold and silver, I found scarce and denied
to many people. Then I began to consider and compare
the value of them which I measured by their service to
men and the virtues which would be found to have
been in them if they were taken away. As a result I
saw clearly that there was a real value in common
things, a fictitious one in those that were scarce.

✴XXXIV✴

EVELYN UNDERHILL wrote: The true mystic who is so
often accused of 'denying the world' is only denying
the narrow and artificial world of self and finding in
exchange the secrets of that mighty universe which he
shares with nature and with God. In the remaking of
his consciousness which follows upon the 'Mystical
awakening', the deep and primal life which he shares
with all creation has been aroused from its sleep. Hence
the barrier between human and non-human life which
makes man a stranger on earth as well as in heaven is
done away.

✴XXXV✴

WALTER HILTON wrote: The true lover thinks that he
is indeed nothing, and that he can indeed do nothing
of himself but is, as it were, a dead thing only supported and borne up by the mercy of God. He sees
clearly that Jesus is all and does all and therefore he
asks for nothing else but the gift of love, for since the
soul sees that his own love is nothing, therefore it
would have his love, for that is sufficient. So he prays
and desires that the love of God should touch him

with his blessed light in order that he might see a
little of him by his gracious presence, for then he
would love him.

WALTER HILTON tells the parable of 'The Pilgrim':
There was a man who had a great desire to go to
Jerusalem and because he did not know the right way,
he sought advice from one whom he hoped knew and
he asked him if there was any passable way there. The
other answered that the way was both long and full of
great difficulties. Indeed there were many ways, that
seemed and promised to lead there but the dangers
were too great. Nevertheless, he knew one way, which
if he would diligently pursue this according to the
directions and marks he would give him, though, he
said, I cannot promise you security from many
frights, beatings and other ill-usage and temptations
of all kinds, if you can have courage and patience
enough to suffer them without quarrelling or resisting
or troubling yourself and so pass on, having only this
in mind and sometimes on your tongue, 'I am nothing,
I have nothing, I desire nothing but to be at Jerusalem',
my life for yours, you will escape safe with your life
and in due time arrive there.

XXXVII

THEN he instructed him: Begin your journey in God's
name, but be sure to go furnished with two necessary
instruments, humility and love. Both are contained in
the forementioned speech, which must always be

ready in your mind: I am nothing, I have nothing, I desire only one thing and that is our Lord Jesus and to be with him in peace at Jerusalem. The meaning and the virtue of these words therefore you must have continually in your thoughts either consciously or unconsciously. Humility says: I am nothing, I have nothing. Love says: I desire nothing but Jesus. From these two companions you must never part nor will they willingly be separated from one another for they agree very lovingly together and the deeper you school yourself in humility the higher you raise yourself in love, and the more you see and feel yourself to be nothing with the more fervent love will you desire Jesus that by him who is all, you may become something. Therefore cast all other things behind you that you may have that which is best of all and so doing you will become a true pilgrim that leaves behind him house and wife and children and friends and goods and makes himself poor and bare of all things that he may go on his journey lightly and merrily without hindrance.

* XXXVIII *

HIS GUIDE warned him: If it shall happen sometimes, as it probably will, that through these temptations and your own frailty you stumble and perhaps fall down, and get some harm thereby, or that you for some time are turned a little out of the right way, as soon as you possibly can come again to your senses, get up again and return to the right way using such remedies for your hurt as the church ordains and do not trouble yourself overmuch or overlong with troubled thoughts about your past misfortune and pain. Stay not in such thoughts for that will do you more harm and give advantage to your enemies. Therefore make haste and continue working again as if nothing had happened. Keep only Jesus in your mind and a desire to gain his love.

* XXXIX *

FURTHER he said: You will often be forced as all other pilgrims are to take refreshments by the way, meat and drink and sleep, yes, and sometimes innocent re-creations. In all these things use discretion and take no heed of foolish scruples about them. Do not fear that they will be much hindrance to you for though they seem to delay you for a while they will help you on and give you strength to walk more courageously for a long time thereafter.

* XL *

FINALLY he gave this warning: At last when your enemies see that your will to Jesus is so strong that you will stop neither for poverty or mischief, for sickness or fancies, for doubts or fears, for life or death nor for sins either but you will go on with that one purpose of seeking the love of Jesus, and nothing else and that you despise and barely notice anything that they say to the contrary, but hold on in your prayer and other spiritual works (yet always with discretion and submission), they will come closer to you than ever before and launch their last and most dangerous assault, and that is to bring in the sight of your mind all your good deeds and virtues showing you that all men praise you and love you and hold you in great veneration for your sanctity. And all this they will do so as to raise vain joy and pride in your heart. But if you regard your life you will hold all this flattery and falsehood to be a deadly poison to your soul mingled with honey, therefore, away with it, cast it from you saying that you will have none of it but that you would be at Jerusalem.

⋆XLI⋆

AELRED wrote: It is clear, unless I am mistaken, that it is not by the motion of the feet but by inclination of the mind that a man journeys away from the highest good. For human pride dwelling long in us destroys the image of God in us. Even so human humility approaching to God by inclination of the mind renews the image in which God created us. Our human love, infected by the poison of lust and miserably ensnared in the sticky birdlime of human pleasure, is always carried down to the depth that is from one vice into another by its own weight. But when true love flows in from above and dissolves by its heat our inborn torpor it rises up to higher things. It puts off the old and puts on the new, it receives the silver wings of the dove with which it flies to that sublime and pure good from which it had its birth.

⋆XLII⋆

THE AUTHOR of *The Cloud of Unknowing* said: Take good care of time, how you spend it, for nothing is more precious than time. In one little moment, short as it is, heaven may be won or lost.

FATHER AUGUSTINE BAKER wrote: If souls would courageously give themselves wholly to God they would find that all things would co-operate not only to their eternal good but even to their present contentment and joy. What contentment can be greater to a soul than to become a true inward friend of God chained to him with a love the like of which never existed between any mortal creatures?

THE POETESS Augusta Drane wrote:

Through the dark night I wander on alone,
And, as one blinded, grope my weary way,
Without a lamp to shed its guiding ray;
I wander on unseen and seeing none,
And caring to behold but only One.

I see not, yet my heart will give me light,
And safer than the noonday sun will guide
To where the Bridegroom waiteth for the Bride;
So walking on in faith and not by sight
I cannot fear but he will guide me right.

HENRY VAUGHAN wrote:

There is in God—some say—
A deep, but dazzling darkness; as men here

Say it is late and dusky, because they
    See not all clear.
O for that Night! where I in Him
Might live invisible and dim!

* XLVI *

T. S. ELIOT wrote: I said to my soul, be still and let the
dark come upon you. Which shall be the darkness of
God.

* XLVII *

THE AUTHOR of *The Cloud* taught: Lift up your hearts
unto God with a humble stirring of love and mean
God himself and not any of the good things which he
gives and mind that you do not let yourself think of
anything but him himself, so that nothing works in
your mind nor your will but only he, and so work that
you forget all the creatures that God ever made and
their works, so that neither your thought nor your
desire is directed or stretched towards any of them
either in general or in particular but let them be and
have no care for them. Do not cease but work therein
until you feel longing, for at first when you do it
you find only a darkness and, as it were, a cloud of
unknowing, you never know what it is except that you
feel in your soul a pure intention reaching towards
God. This darkness and this cloud is, whatever you
do, between you and your God and prevents you
from seeing him clearly by light of rational understanding or feeling the sweetness of this love in your
affection. Therefore prepare yourself to stay in this

darkness as long as you may, evermore crying after him whom you love. For if ever you see him or feel him in this life, it must always be in this cloud and this darkness, and if you work busily as I tell you, I trust that you will come to this by His mercy.

★ XLVIII ★

LOVE makes the loving one like that which he loves.

★ XLIX ★

THE AUTHOR of *The Cloud* gave this warning: For the love of God take care in this work that you do not strain the heart in your breast too violently nor without due measure but work more with earnestness than with mere strength. For as you are more earnest so you are more humble and spiritual, but the more violent you are the more bodily and bestial, for such violent strainings hurt the silly soul sorely and make it fester in fantasies feigned by fiends. Therefore beware of this bestial violence and learn to love earnestly with a gentle and demure behaviour both in body and soul and await courteously and humbly the will of our Lord and do not snatch over hastily like a greedy greyhound however hungry you may be.

★ L ★

THE AUTHOR of *The Cloud* further gives a severe warning on taking the terms used by writers on mysticism too literally: The madness [of one who seeks mysticism in the wrong way] happens in this way.

They read and hear it rightly said that they should leave outward workings with their minds and work inwardly. But since they do not know what inward working means, naturally they work wrongly. For they turn their bodily mind inwards towards the body against the course of nature, and strain themselves as if they would see inwardly with their bodily eyes, and hear inwardly with their ears, and so on with all their faculties, smell, taste and feeling. They turn them inwards and so go against what is natural and by this behaviour they strain their imagination so indiscreetly that at last they turn the brains in their heads. Then at once the devil has power to give them delusions of false light or sounds or sweet smells in their noses, wonderful tastes in their mouths and many strange feelings of heat and burning in their breasts, in their backs, in their bowels and in their privy parts.

★LI★

THE AUTHOR of *The Cloud* tells how the soul may come to know God: All reasonable creatures, angels and men, have in them, each one individually, one principal working power which is called knowing power and another principal working power which is called loving power. Concerning the two powers, to the first, that is knowing power, God who is the maker of them is for ever incomprehensible. But to the second, that is loving power, in each one differently he is entirely comprehensible to the full. Insomuch that one loving soul alone by itself, by virtue of love, can comprehend in itself him who is able to fill full—and much more without comparison—all the souls and angels that ever may be and this is a marvellous miracle of love that will never end. Forever he shall do it and never shall he cease from doing it.

JOHN SMITH the Platonist wrote: The best and truest knowledge of God is not that which is wrought out by labour and sweat of the brain but that which is kindled within us by a heavenly warmth in our hearts. As in the natural body it is the heart that sends up the good blood and warm spirits into the head, whereby it is best enabled to perform its several functions. So that which enables us to know and understand aright in the things of God must be a living principle of holiness within us. When the tree of knowledge is not planted by the tree of life, and does not suck up sap from it, it may as well be fruitful with evil as with good, and bring forth bitter fruits as well as sweet. If we would indeed have our knowledge thrive and flourish we must water the tender plants of it with holiness.

GEORGE HERBERT wrote:

> Lord Jesu, thou didst bow
> Thy dying head upon the tree
>   Oh be not now
>   More dead to me!
> Lord, hear! Shall he that made the ear
>   Not hear?

Behold thy dust doth stir;
It moves, it creeps, it aims at thee:
  Wilt thou defer
  To succour me,
Thy pile of dust, wherein each crumb
  Says, 'Come'.

⋆ LIV ⋆

WE READ in *The Cloud*: For charity means nothing
else to your understanding but love of God for
himself above all creatures and of men even as yourself for God's sake. It seems very good that in this work
God is loved for himself above all creatures. For as has
been said before, the substance of this work is nothing
else but a pure intention directed towards God for
himself. A pure intention I call it because in this work
the perfect apprentice asks neither for release from
pain nor increase of reward but, to put it shortly,
nothing but God himself. He neither cares nor notices
whether he is in pain or bliss but only that the will of
him he loves is fulfilled, and so it is seen that in this
work God is perfectly loved for himself and that above
all creatures. For in this work a perfect worker will not
allow the thought of the holiest creature that ever God
made, to have a share with him. And that in this, the
second and lower branch of charity to your fellow
Christian, is truly and perfectly fulfilled as seen by the
proof. For in this work a perfect worker has no special
regard for any man for himself whether he is a relation
or stranger, friend or foe, for all men alike seem related
to him and no man a stranger. All men seem to him to

42

be his friends and none his foes. Insomuch that he thinks that all those who give him pain and cause him trouble in this life are his full and special friends, and he is stirred to wish them as much good as he would the closest friend that he has.

* L V *

RICHARD ROLLE wrote: There are three degrees of love of which I tell you, for I wish that you might win to the highest. The first degree is called insuperable, the second inseparable, the third singular. Your love is insuperable when nothing that is contrary to God's love overcomes it, when it is stalwart against all temptations and stable whether you are at ease or in anguish, in health or in sickness. So that you think you would not for the whole world provoke God to wrath at any time, and you would suffer all the pain and woe that could happen to any creature rather than do anything that would displease him. So love is insuperable when nothing can bring it down but it springs up on high. Blessed is he or she who is in this degree, but yet they are more blessed who might hold onto this degree and attain to the other that is inseparable.

Your love is inseparable when all your heart and all your thought and all your might are so wholly, so entirely and so perfectly fastened, set and fixed in our Lord Jesus, that your thought never leaves him and never departs from him. When you can at no time forget him whatever you do or say, then is your love inseparable. Much grace have they that are in this degree of love.

The third degree is the highest and the most wonderful to win, that which is called singular, for it has no equal. Singular love is when all comfort and solace is closed out of the heart except Jesus Christ alone. Other joys attract it not at all, for his sweetness is so comforting and lasting, and his love so burning and gladdening, that he or she who is in this degree may feel the fire of love burning in their soul as clearly as you may feel your finger burn if you put it in the fire. But that fire, if it is hot, is so delightful and wonderful that I cannot tell of it.

★ LVI ★

THE AUTHOR of *The Cloud* wrote: Of one thing I warn you, whoever you are that read or hear this writing.

I refer to the place where I make the difference between those who have been called to salvation and those who have been called to perfection. In whichever sphere you feel your calling is, see that you neither judge or discuss the deeds of God or of any other men than yourself. For example, who he stirs and calls to perfection and who he does not call, or the shortness of time, or why he calls one rather than another. If you do not wish to err see that you do not judge but only hear and understand. If you are called, give praise to God and pray that you may not fall. And if you are not called, pray humbly to God that he may call you when it is his will. But do not try to teach him what he shall do. Let him alone. He is mighty and wise and willing enough to do the best for you and all that love him.

WILLIAM LAW said: Now there is but one possible way for a man to attain to salvation. There is not one for the Jew, another for the Christian and a third for the heathen. No! God is one, human nature is one, salvation is one and the way to it is one; and that is the desire of the soul turned towards God. When the desire is alive and breaks forth in any creature under heaven, then the lost sheep is found and the shepherd has it on his shoulder.

GEORGE HERBERT taught:

> Teach me, my God and King,
> In all things Thee to see
> And what I do in any thing
> To do it as for Thee.

OUR LORD said to Julian of Norwich in her vision: I will that you wisely know your penance and you shall see in truth that all your living is penance profitable.

WALTER HILTON gave the following advice to a man living in the world as to how to combine the active and the contemplative life: I well know the desire of your heart that you yearn greatly to serve our Lord in spiritual occupation without the interference and trouble of worldly business so that you might by grace come to more knowledge and spiritual feeling of God and spiritual things. This desire is, I believe, good and from God for it is love specially directed towards him. Nevertheless, it is to be restrained and ruled by discretion as regards your outward doings in accordance with the state in which you are. For love unruled turns sometimes into vice. So this love and this desire that our Lord in his mercy has given to you must be ruled and ordered as to the manner in which you shall pursue it in accordance with that which your station in life demands and in accordance with the way you used to live before this and also in accordance with the grace that you now have. You must not entirely follow your desire and leave the occupation and business of this world which you need to use in ruling of yourself and all others that are in your keeping, and give yourself wholly to the spiritual occupations of prayer and meditation as if you were a monk or a friar or some other man that was not bound to the world by children and servants as you are. For this is not your part and if you do so you offend against the rule of love. But if you should utterly leave spiritual occupation now, after the grace that God has given you, and settle down wholly to the business of the world and to carrying out of the works of active life as fully as another that never felt devotion, you lose the rule of love. For your state demands that you do both at different times. You must mix the works of active life with the spiritual works of contemplative life and then you are doing well.

* LXI *

WALTER HILTON gave the men in this world the

following consolation: It may happen sometimes that the more troubled you have been outwardly with active works the more burning the desire you shall have towards God and, by the grace of our Lord, the clearer sight of spiritual things in your devotions when you come to them. It is as if you have a little coal and you wish to make a fire with it and make it burn. You would first lay sticks on it and cover over the coal and although it seemed for a time that you would put the fire out with the sticks nonetheless when you have waited a while and then blown a little, there springs up a great flame of fire for the sticks are turned into fire. So it is with spiritual things: your will and your desire that you have for God is, as it were, a little coal of fire in your soul. For it gives you some spiritual heat and spiritual light, but it is very little, for often it grows cold and turns to bodily rest and sometimes turns into idleness, therefore it is good that you should put sticks on it; these are the good works of active life. And if it seems that for a time these works hinder your desire so that it may not be as clean and as fervent as you would have it, do not be too daunted on this account but wait and suffer a while and go and blow at the fire. That is, first do your works and then go alone to your prayers and your meditations and lift up your heart to God and pray him of his goodness that will accept the works that you do for his pleasure.

LXII

WALTER HILTON wrote: Furthermore I say unto you, when you pray or think or do any other act, either well

47

through grace or ill through your own frailty, and everything you feel, see, hear and smell or taste, either outwardly by your bodily senses or inwardly in your imagination or know or feel through your reason, bring them all within the truth and rules of the Holy Church. Cast all into the mortar of humility and break it small with the pestle of the fear of God and throw the powder of all this into the fire of desire and offer it thus to God. I tell you truly that your offering shall be well pleasing in the sight of your Lord Jesus and the smoke of your fire smell sweet to your Lord Jesus.

✴ LXIII ✴

GEORGE HERBERT wrote:

Love bade me welcome: yet my soul drew back,
    Guilty of dust and sin.
But quick-eyed Love, observing me grow slack
    From my first entrance in,
Drew nearer to me, sweetly questioning
    If I lack'd any thing.

'A guest', I answered, 'worthy to be here':
    Love said, 'You shall be he'.
'I the unkind, ungrateful? Ah my dear
    I cannot look on thee.'
Love took my hand, and smiling did reply,
    'Who made the eyes but I?'

'Truth Lord, but I have marr'd them; let my shame
    Go where it doth deserve'.
'And know you not', says Love, 'who bore the blame?'
    'My dear, then I will serve.'

'You must sit down', says Love, 'and taste my meat':
    So I did sit and eat.

WILLIAM LAW wrote in one of his letters: May not a person renounce all worldly business purely for the sake of devotion and give himself wholly up to spiritual exercises? He may certainly renounce what we generally mean by worldly business, trades, etc., for the sake of a greater opportunity for devotion, etc. But then although this or that trade or place may be renounced for this end yet he that renounces humble, charitable and painful labour in order to advance in devotion seems to mistake the point and to renounce the very best preservatives of true devotion.

THE AUTHOR of *The Cloud* writes out of his own experience: And as God will answer for us in spirit so he will stir up other men in spirit to give us the things we need that belong to this life like meat and clothes and all other such things, if he sees that we will not leave the work of love to busy ourselves about them. This I say in contradiction of their error who say that it is not allowable for men to set themselves to serve God in contemplative life unless beforehand they have made sure of securing their bodily necessities. For they say 'God sends the cow but not by the horn'[1] and truly they speak wrongfully of God as they well

[1] A medieval proverb meaning much the same as God helps those who help themselves.

know. For trust steadfastly, you, whoever you may be, who truly turns from the world to God, that God will send you one of these two things without you busying yourself with it: either abundance of necessities or else strength of body and patience of spirit to bear your needs. What does it matter which a man has? For it is all one to true contemplatives and whoever doubts this, either the devil is in his heart and robs him of belief or else he is not truly turned to God as he should be, whoever he is and whatever ingenious and holy arguments he may bring against it.

∗ LXVI ∗

GOD provides for him who trusts.

∗ LXVII ∗

WALTER HILTON says of prayer: Prayer is profitable and helpful to use so as to get cleanness of heart by destroying sin and bringing in virtues, not so as to make known to our Lord in your prayer what you desire, for he knows well enough what you need, but to make yourself able and ready by your prayer to receive as a clean vessel the grace that our Lord will freely give you. This grace may not be felt until you are tested and purified by the fire of desire in devout prayer. For although prayer is not the cause of our Lord giving grace it is nevertheless the way by which grace given freely comes to a soul.

∗ LXVIII ∗

THE AUTHOR of *The Cloud* teaches on prayer: Just as

the meditations of those who continually follow this form of spiritual life always rise suddenly without any cause so do their special prayers. If these are in words, which they seldom are, then let them be in very few words, yes, always the fewer the better. If it is a little word of one syllable I think that it is better than if it is of two, and more according to the work of the spirit since a spiritual worker in this work should evermore be in the highest and topmost peak of spiritual life. That this is so you may see in the course of ordinary life. A man or woman unexpectedly frightened by fire or a man's death or anything else of this sort suddenly is so driven by the fullness of his spirit that he is immediately forced to cry out or call for help. See how he does it: certainly not in many words nor in a word of two syllables. Why is that? Because he thinks it will take too long to declare his need and trouble of spirit and therefore he bursts out vehemently from the depth of his soul and cries out but one little word of one syllable, such as the word 'fire' or 'help'. Just as this little word 'fire' stirs men up more, and more quickly pierces the ears of those that hear, so a little word of one syllable, when it is not only spoken or thought but inwardly meant in the depth of the spirit, will more surely pierce the ears of Almighty God than any long series of psalms unmindfully mumbled. That is why it is written that a short prayer pierces heaven.

* LXIX *

WALTER HILTON said: When you do a good deed or pray or think of God, do not have in your heart doubt whether you desire or not, for the deed shows your desire. Some are unwise and think that they desire God only if they are always crying to God with words in their mouths or else in their hearts as if they said: 'O Lord bring me to your bliss'; 'Lord make me safe' and other such words. These words are good whether they are said with the mouth or formed in the heart for they stir up a man's heart to the desiring of God. But nevertheless without any such words a clean thought of God or any spiritual thing—such as the virtues, or the manhood of Christ, or the joys of heaven, or the understanding of the holy writ with love—may be better than such words. For a clean thought of God is a true desire of him and the more spiritual that thought is, the more is your desire.

★ LXX ★

FATHER BAKER wrote: The smallest act of love and service to God performed with perfect self-denial is more acceptable and precious in his eyes, than the working of a thousand miracles or the conversion of nations, if in these there are mixed motives.

★ LXXI ★

WILLIAM LAW writes: When this state of fervour has done its work, has melted away all passions and affections and has left no inclination in the soul but to delight in God alone, then its prayer changes again. It is now so near God, has found such union with him that it does not so much pray as live in God. Its prayer is not any particular action, it is not the work of any particular facility nor confined to any times or words or place but is the work of his whole being which continually stands in fullness of faith, in purity of love, in absolute resignation to do and to be what his Beloved pleases. This is the last state of the spirit of prayer, and its highest union with God in this life.

⋆ LXXII ⋆

FATHER AUGUSTINE BAKER teaches: An imperfect, interrupted prayer made with resignation in the midst of pains or troubles sent by God is perhaps more efficacious in procuring the good of the soul than the highest forms of prayer exercised otherwise. It is no great matter that the soul herself does not distinctly or clearly see how her present suffering (external or internal) may be profitable to her; she is to refer all things to the infinite goodness and wisdom of God, who can bring light out of darkness. Therefore she must be contented (if such be his will) to be blindfolded and humbly to remain in her simplicity and in reverential awe and admiration of the inscrutable ways of divine providence.

⋆ LXXIII ⋆

FATHER BAKER said: Those whose sufferings are merely from outward pains, without sickness, may have their prayers altered for the better by means of such pains which themselves may prove a very profitable prayer, if the patient with quietness and submission to the divine will offer such pains continually to God.

WE FIND in the *Ancrene Riwle:* Let an anchoress keep silence as much as ever she can and may. Let her not have the hen's nature, which when she has laid cannot help cackling. And what does she get from it? Straightway comes the crow and robs her of her eggs and devours all that from which she should have hatched live chicks. A wretched pedlar makes more noise over crying his soap than a rich cloth merchant over all his costly wares.

THE *Ancrene Riwle* goes on: Long silence and well kept forces the thoughts up towards Heaven. Just as you may see that water—when men dam it and block it before a spring so that it may not flow downwards— is forced to climb upwards again. In this way we must dam our words and block our thoughts for we would wish them to climb upwards towards heaven and not flow downwards and scatter over the world as does much chatter. But when you must needs speak, raise up the floodgates of your mouth a little as men do at the mill and soon let them down again.

JOHN SMITH said: All self-seeking and self-love imprison the soul and confine it to its own home. The mind of a good man is too noble; too big for such a self centred life. He has learned to despise his own being in comparison to that uncreated Beauty and Goodness which is so infinitely transcendent to himself or to any created thing. He reckons upon his choice and best affections and designs as too choice and precious a treasure to be spent on such a sorry thing as himself or upon anything else but God himself.

WILLIAM LAW said: But the one true way of dying to self is most simple and plain. It wants no arts or methods, no cells, monasteries or pilgrimages, it is equally practicable in everybody, it is always at hand, it meets you in every thing, it is free from all deceit and never without success. If you ask what is this one true, simple, plain, immediate and unerring way? It is the way of patience, meekness, humility, and resignation to God.

THERE IS in spiritual life no pretence to strange novelties and wonders. Divine love is all; it begins with love and resignation and there it ends likewise.

GEORGE HERBERT wrote:

> Though I fail, I weep:
> Though I halt in pace,
>   Yet I creep
> To the throne of grace.
>
> Then let wrath remove:
> Love will do the deed;
>   For with love
> Stony hearts will bleed.

Love is swift of foot;
Love's a man of war,
　And can shoot,
And can hit from far.

Who can 'scape his bow?
That which wrought on thee,
　Brought thee low,
Needs must work on me.

LXXX

THOMAS TRAHERNE has in his *Meditations*: No man loves, if he does not love another more than himself. In ordinary instances this is apparent. If you come into an orchard with a person you love and there is but one ripe cherry you offer it to the other. If two lovers delight in the same piece of meat, each takes pleasure in the other having it and values the beloved's satisfaction more than his own. What ails men, that they do not see it? In greater cases this is evident. A mother runs upon a sword to save her beloved. A father leaps into the fire to fetch out his beloved. Love brought Christ from heaven to die for his beloved. It is in the nature of love to despise itself and to think only of its beloved's welfare. It is not true love if it is otherwise. I am sure nothing is more acceptable to God, than to love others so as to be willing to give even one's own soul for their benefit and welfare.

LXXXI

WALTER HILTON wrote: You must never condemn

other men nor conceive against them wilfully any evil suspicions. But you shall love them and not see any fault in them and hold in high regard those that lead an active life in the world and suffer many troubles and temptations of which you, sitting in your house, feel nothing. They have much work and worry for their own and other men's livelihood (and many of them would much rather serve God if they might, as you do, in bodily rest). Nevertheless they, in their worldly business, avoid many sins into which you, if you were in their circumstances, would fall and they do many good deeds which you would not do. There is no doubt that many do this (but which they are you do not know) and therefore you shall hold them all in high regard and esteem them all in your heart above yourself as your superiors, and cast yourself down under their feet so that you may be the vilest and lowest in your own sight. There is no dread or peril for you however much you lower yourself beneath all others, for it may be that in God's sight you have more grace than others. But it is perilous for you to hold yourself high and wilfully lift yourself in your thoughts above any other man, although he were the most wretched and most sinful villain that there is on earth. For our Lord says: He that makes himself high shall be made low, and he who makes himself low shall be made high.

∗ LXXXII ∗

RICHARD ROLLE said: The righteous are humble, truly loving and neglect nothing. They, although they exist in the highest state of perfection, bear themselves very humbly both in mind and in deed. He who is a true lover says within himself: All excel me in contempt of the world, in hate of sin, in desire for the heavenly kingdom, in the sweetness and fervour of the love of Christ, in charity towards their neighbour. When I consider the noble lives of so many compared with my own, I am, as it were, reduced to nothing and as becomes one so weak, give place to all.

* LXXXIII *

THE AUTHOR of *The Cloud* wrote: You who set out to be a contemplative, choose rather to be humbled because of the wonderful height and the worthiness of God which is perfect, than because of your own wretchedness which is imperfect. That is to say, see that your special regard is more to the worthiness of God than to your wretchedness. For to them that are perfectly humbled nothing shall be lacking, neither spiritual things nor bodily, because they have God in whom is all plenty, and who so has him needs nothing else in life.

* LXXXIV *

THE POET T. S. Eliot wrote:

> Do not let me hear
> Of the wisdom of the old men, but rather of their folly,
> Their fear of fear and frenzy, their fear of possession,
> Of belonging to another, or others, or to God.
> The only wisdom we can hope to acquire
> Is the wisdom of humility: humility is endless.

REAL DETACHMENT means the death of preferences of all kinds, even of those which seem to other men the very proofs of virtue and fine taste.

WILLIAM LAW said: You need not therefore run here or there saying: Where is Christ? For behold the Word, which is the Wisdom of God, is in your heart. It is there as the speaking Word of God in your soul, and as soon as you are ready to hear, the eternal speaking Word will speak wisdom and love in your inward parts and bring forth the birth of Christ with all His holy nature, spirit, and character within you. Hence it was, that so many eminent spirits, partakers of divine life, have appeared in so many parts of the heathen world; glorious names, sons of wisdom, that shone as lights hung out by God in the midst of idolatrous darkness. These apostles had not the law, nor written gospel to urge upon their hearers, yet having turned to God, they found and preached the gospel that was written in their hearts.

AELRED tells us: Take good note, that Solomon does not say: He who has riches, but he says: He who loves riches shall get no fruit from them. For certainly all the elect, even if they should chance to have riches, do not love them and so do not seek their rest in them. They listen to the Apostle's instruction to the rich not

to be proud-minded nor put their hope in the un-
certainty of riches, but they distribute them freely and
share them and lay up for themselves a good founda-
tion that they may lay hold of true life. From their
riches they not only receive fruit but they shall surely
hear from the Lord: Come blessed of my Father, for
I was hungry and ye gave me to eat, etc. Indeed these
do not strive for the acquiring of riches, fearing as the
Apostle says: Those who wish to become rich fall into
the devil's snare. The vain care of preserving their
wealth does not torment them, remembering the
more deeply the promise of our Lord who so forbade
anxiety and promised all things that were necessary.
Lastly they do not complain if they lose their wealth,
rather they accept with joy the taking away of their
goods, considering that they have a better and more
enduring livelihood.

★ LXXXVIII ★

FATHER BAKER said: Even as the soul may resign herself
to sickness, pain, want, dishonour, so she may also for
the glory of God resign herself to health, pleasures,
riches, honour, intending if God's will be such to
accept these also and to employ them only in his glory
and not to the satisfaction of corrupt nature, not
diminishing, but rather increasing humility and divine
love by them.

★ LXXXIX ★

FATHER BAKER said: It is the nature of a spiritual life to

make good use both of prosperity and adversity in all things, renouncing all self-seeking and having an eye to God. Indeed considering our frailty and our inclination to be corrupted by prosperity, adversity is far more secure and profitable to us.

★ X C ★

THOMAS TRAHERNE wrote in his *Meditations*: It was his wisdom made you need the sun. It was his goodness made you need the sea. Understand what it is you need so that you may appreciate them. Think how much you need them, for it is from this they derive their value. Suppose the sun was extinguished; or the sea were dry. There would be no light, no beauty, no warmth, no fruits, no flowers, no pleasant gardens, feasts or prospects, no wine, no oil, no bread, no life, no motion. Would you not give all the gold and silver in the Indies for such a treasure? Prize it now you have it.

★ X C I ★

MARGERY KEMPE said to our Lord Jesus in her visions: Ah, Lord Jesus, since it was so sweet to weep for your love on earth I know right well that it will be right joyful to be with you in Heaven. Therefore, Lord, I pray you let me never have other joy on earth but mourning and weeping for your love. For I think, Lord, though I were in hell, if I might weep and mourn for your love as I do here, hell would not annoy me but would be a kind of heaven, for your love puts away all kinds of fear of our spiritual enemy. I would

61

rather be there as long as you wish and please you than be in this world and displease you, then Lord as you will it so let it be.

THE LORD said to Margery Kempe: You say that though I stood before you in my own person and said that you should never have my love nor ever come to heaven nor ever see my face, yet you say, daughter, that you would never forsake me on earth nor ever love me less nor ever make it less your business to please me though you should lie in hell without end, for you cannot forgo my love on earth, nor can you have any other comfort but me only, who am your God and am all joy and bliss to you. Therefore I must say to you, dear daughter, that it is impossible that any such soul should be damned or parted from me, who has such great meekness and love towards me.

COVENTRY PATMORE wrote: The spirit of man is like a kite which rises by means of those very forces which seem to oppose its rise: the tie that joins it to the earth, the opposing winds of temptation and the load of earth-born affections which it carries with it into the sky.

IN THE *Ancrene Riwle* we read: The greater and higher the hill, the more windy it is. So as the hill of holy and exhalted life is greater and higher so do the puffs of the fiend—which are the winds of temptation—blow on it more strongly and more often.

★ XCV ★

IN THE *Ancrene Riwle* we read: A tower is not attacked, nor a castle nor a city when it has already been taken, so Hell's warrior assails with temptation no one who has already fallen into his hands, but attacks those that are not his.

★ XCVI ★

COVENTRY PATMORE wrote: Remember that no struggle however faint and brief is really unsuccessful. If we do not gain the victory, at least we diminish the future pain of defeat. Remember also that to rise and go on fighting after repeated disgrace and failure is victory over all three enemies of the soul: sloth, pride and despair.

★ XCVII ★

FATHER BAKER wrote: We must not voluntarily seek temptations. For he that loves danger shall perish therein, says the wise man. God will not deny spiritual strength to resist and make good use of temptations that by his providence befall us, yes though it was by some previous fault and negligence of ours that they befell us. But he has made no promise to secure us in a danger into which we voluntarily run.

63

FATHER BAKER wrote: Harpius said to one of those who complained that they lacked opportunity to exercise resignation: You deceive yourself through pride. God sees that as yet you are not ready nor strong enough for extraordinary trials. For if he saw that you were, he would not fail to furnish you with opportunities.

JULIAN OF NORWICH wrote: After this the Lord brought to my mind the longing that I had had for Him before. And I saw that nothing hindered me but sin and I saw that it was so generally in all of us, and I thought: If sin had not been, we would have been clean and like our Lord as he made us. But Jesus, who in this vision told me about everything that I needed to know, answered as follows and said: It is necessary that there shall be sin, but all shall be well, and all shall be well and all manner of things shall be well. And in these words I saw a marvellous high secret hid in God, a secret he will openly make known to us in heaven, and knowing this we shall truly see the cause for which he allowed sin to come and in this sight we shall have endless joy in our Lord God.

THOMAS TRAHERNE wrote: To know God is life eternal. To know God is to know goodness; it is to see the beauty of infinite love; to see it attended with almighty power and eternal wisdom. It is to see the king of heaven and earth take infinite delight in giving. He is not an object of terror, but delight. To know him therefore as he is, is to frame the most beautiful idea in all worlds. He delights in our happiness more than we do. An infinite Lord, who, having all riches, honours and pleasures in his own hand, is infinitely willing to give them unto me.

★ CI ★

JULIAN OF NORWICH wrote: And thus throughout this vision I was obliged to see and know that we are sinners and do many evil things that we ought to leave undone and leave many good deeds undone that we ought to do. Therefore we deserve pain and anger. Not withstanding all this I saw unequivocally that our Lord was never angry nor ever shall be, for he is God: Good, Life, Truth, Love, Peace. His love and his unity do not allow him to be angry. For I saw truly that it was against the nature of his wisdom and against the nature of his goodness. God is the goodness that may not be angry for he is nothing else but goodness.

★ CII ★

JULIAN OF NORWICH wrote: I saw clearly that where the Lord appears peace comes and anger has no place.

★ CIII ★

WILLIAM LAW said: God is an utter infinity of love, wisdom and goodness. He ever was and ever will be

65

one and the same unchangeable will to goodness and works of love, as incapable of any feeling of wrath or acting under its influence, as of falling under pain or darkness and acting under their direction.

★ CIV ★

JULIAN OF NORWICH had the following vision: For the first time I saw two people in bodily likeness, a lord and a servant and God gave me spiritual understanding of it. The lord sits quietly at rest and in peace, the servant stands by in front of his lord, reverently, ready to do his lord's will. The lord looks upon the servant very lovingly and sweetly and with a gentle word sends him to a certain place to do his will. The servant not only goes but starts at once and runs with great haste in his desire to do his lord's will and in doing so falls into a ravine and hurts himself badly and then he moans and groans and wails and writhes but he can neither get up or help himself in any way. And in all this the worst misfortune that befell him, as I saw it, was the lack of all comfort, as a man who was feeble and foolish for the time being, he focused his attention on his feelings and suffered a great deal. I marvelled how meekly this servant bore all his sufferings and I carefully sought to learn if I could see any fault in him, or if the lord should hold him in any way to blame. And truly I could find no fault for only his goodwill and his great longing were the cause of his falling and he was still as ready and good inwardly as when he stood before his lord ready to do his will. And it is even thus that his loving lord always very tenderly regards him. Then it was as if his courteous lord were saying: See what harm and discomfort my beloved servant has received in my service and for love of me, yes, and on account of his goodwill. Is it not right that I reward him for his fright and fear and his hurt and his injury and all his suffering and not only this but must I not give him a gift that is better for him and more honourable than his health would have been; otherwise I would show him no gratitude?

★ CV ★

WE READ in the *Ancrene Riwle*: Now take care and learn by many examples how good is unity of love and oneness of heart. For surely you know that when men fight in strong armies they who keep themselves firmly united together can in no way be discomforted and overcome. It is the same in the spiritual fight against the devil. His whole intention is to disunite hearts and to take away the love that binds men together. For when love fails and they are divided, the devil at once puts himself between them and slays on every side. Dumb beasts have this instinct that when they are attacked by a wolf or a lion the whole herd crowd together and make a shield of themself each for the other, and are safe for the time being. But if any hapless creature goes out on its own it is at once savaged. The third example is that if a man goes alone on a slippery path he soon slips and falls, but when many go together they each hold the others' hands and if any of them begins to slip the others hold him up so that he does not quite fall, and if they grow tired each one is supported by the others. In the same way in a strong wind or a swift current they that must wade over—if there are many—hold each others' hands and if one is separated he is soon swept away and perishes. We know too well that the path through this world is slippery and the wind and the currents are strong. There is great need that each one holds to the other with assiduous prayer and lovingly holds the other's hand, for as Solomon says: Woe to him that is alone for when he has fallen he has none to raise him up. None is alone that has God for a companion as has each one that has true love in his heart.

★ CVI ★

WE READ in the *Ancrene Riwle*: If we truly love God we ought to prefer to lose our great reward in heaven to committing one sin, however slight, for the truly righteous man seeks no reward for his righteousness but the friendship of God, because he is God. It is always better therefore to suffer torment than even once willingly and knowingly to be led from righteousness to iniquity.

★ CVII ★

WE READ in the *Ancrene Riwle*: Think yet again what is a word but wind? Too shallowly is she planted whom the puff of a word may uproot and cast down into sin. Who then would not feel wonder at an anchoress whom the wind of a word uproots? Again does she not show that she is but dust, an unstable thing that by one little wind of a word can be blown about and provoked? That same puff of wind if you cast it under your feet would bear you upwards towards the bliss of heaven. And now there is much reason to wonder at our great lack of restraint. We cannot endure the wind of a word that bears us toward heaven but are furious with those that we ought to thank as doing us a great service though it is against their will.

★ CVIII ★

THE *Ancrene Riwle* tells the following story: A man lay in prison who owed a large ransom and in no way could or might he get out—unless it were to be hanged —until he had paid his ransom in full. Would he not be very thankful to a man who cast upon him a purse full of coins wherewith to pay his debt, set him free and release him from pain, although he threw it very hard against his heart? All the pain and all the soreness would be forgotten and forgiven for gladness. In the same way we are all in prison here and owe God great debts for our sins. We say to him in the Lord's prayer: Lord forgive us our debts even as we forgive our debtors. Should any wrong be done to us either by word or deed that is the ransom that shall set us free and acquit us of our debts—that is our sins—to our Lord. For without payment no one is taken out of prison except to be hanged either in purgatory or in the pains of hell.

★ CIX ★

WE READ in the *Ancrene Riwle*: If anyone speaks ill of

you or uses you ill, know and understand that he is your file such as metalworkers use and files away all your rust and all the roughness of your sin. He wears himself away, alas, as does a file but he makes you smooth and burnishes your soul.

⋆ CX ⋆

WE READ in the *Ancrene Riwle*: Think how the good holy man in *The Lives of the Fathers* kissed and blessed the cruel hand that had harmed him and said earnestly as he kissed it tenderly: Ever blessed be his hand for it has prepared for me the bliss of heaven. And you should say also of the hand that ill uses you and the mouth also that speaks ill of you: Blessed be your mouth for you make an instrument of it wherewith I may fashion and increase my crown. Welcome is it to me for my good, woeful is it to me for your evil, for you do me good and harm yourself.

⋆ CXI ⋆

WE READ in the *Ancrene Riwle*: Would the chalice that was melted in the fire and made to boil violently and afterwards fashioned with many blows and much polishing into such a beautiful form for the service of God, curse the cleansing fire and the hands of its maker if it could speak? The whole world is God's smithy wherein he forges his elect. Would you wish that God had no fire in his smithy, nor bellows nor hammers? Fire—that is shame and pain, the bellows—that is those that speak evil of you, your hammers—that is those that do you harm.

70

JULIAN OF NORWICH said: I now see how our Lord rejoiced in the misfortunes of his servants, but with pity and compassion. On each person that he loves, that he may bring them to bliss, he lays something that is no fault in his sight whereby they are blamed and despised in this world; scorned, mocked and outcast. This he does to prevent the harm that they would suffer from the pomp and vainglory of this wretched life and to make their way ready for them to come to heaven and call them to his everlasting bliss. For, he says, I will wholly break you of your empty affections and your vicious pride and after that I shall gather you together and make you gentle and humble, clean and holy by uniting with me.

JULIAN OF NORWICH said: I saw that all the fond and loving compassion that a man has for his fellow-Christians, it is Christ in him.

ONCE when Margery Kempe was at Canterbury and had been greatly despised and reproved because she wept so much, she told the following tale: There was once a man who had sinned greatly against God and when he was shriven his confessor enjoined him, as part of his penance, that he should, for a year, hire men to chide him and reprove him for his sins and that he should give them silver for their labour. One day he came among many great men, such as now are here,

God save you all, and stood among them, as I do now among you, and they reproved him, as you do me, but the man laughed and smiled and was in good spirits at their words. The greatest master amongst them said to the man: Why are you laughing, you rogue, you are greatly despised. Ah Sir, I have good cause to laugh for I have for many days paid silver from my purse and hired men to chide me for the remission of my sins and today I have kept my silver in my purse. I thank you all. Just so I say to you worshipful sirs, while I was at home in my own country, day-by-day I sorrowed with great weeping and mourning that I had no shame, scorn and reproof as I deserved. I thank you all sirs greatly for what both morning and afternoon I have had in fair measure this day, blessed be God for it.

⋆ CXV ⋆

HENRY VAUGHAN wrote on 'Affliction':

Peace! peace! it is not so. Thou dost miscall
Thy physic; pills that change
The sick accessions into settled health;
This is the great elixir, that turns gall
To wine and sweetness, poverty to wealth;
And brings man home when he doth range.
Did not He, who ordained day,
   Ordain night too?
Sickness is wholesome, and crosses are but curbs
To check the mule, unruly man;
They are heaven's husbandry, the famous fan,
Purging the floor which chaff disturbs.

Were all the year one constant sunshine, we
   Should have no flowers;
All would be drought and leanness; not a tree
   Would make us bowers.

⋆ CXVI ⋆

CORN is cleaned by the wind, the soul by chastening.

⋆ CXVII ⋆

COVENTRY PATMORE wrote: To him who waits, all things reveal themselves, so long as he has the courage not to deny in the darkness what he has seen in the light.

⋆ CXVIII ⋆

RICHARD SPENDER, the poet killed in the Second World War, wrote:

Is this sorrow, God, this sickness
The price we must pay?
Is this unbounded emptiness, O God, this heart
   wringing,
The sum that we must render
For that one, dear, treasured glimpse
Of High Eternity?
Yes God!
For that swift flight beyond the earth-bound clouds
Would I again pay tears and weariness,
For one bright flash of Heaven-born flame
Would I again fall burnt and torn to earth.

That soaring through the rack and grey-scarfed night
Was worth the unrelaxing frown of tight-lipped
   Death.
But God, of Thy mercy, grant, O Everlasting
More star-fired sight, more flame, O Lofty One, more
   light!

* CXIX *

IN THE *Ancrene Riwle* we read: Our Lord, when he
allows us to be tempted, plays with us as a mother
with her darling child. She flies from him and hides
herself and lets him sit alone and look anxiously about
and cry: Mummy, Mummy, and weep a short while.
Then she leaps out laughing with her arms outstretched
and clasps him and kisses him and wipes his eyes. Even
so our Lord sometimes leaves us alone for a while and
withdraws his grace, comfort and support, so that we
can find no sweetness in any good that we do nor
satisfaction in our heart. Yet at that very moment he
does not love any the less but he acts from the great
love that he has for us.

* CXX *

WE READ in the *Ancrene Riwle*: There are six reasons
why God, for our good, sometimes withdraws himself. The first is that we should not become proud.
Another, that we may know our own feebleness, our
great infirmity, and our weakness. When two people
are carrying a burden between them and one of them

74

drops it, then the one who is still holding it up will feel the whole weight. Even so, at the time when God is bearing your temptation with you, you never know how heavy it is and therefore sometimes he leaves you alone so that you may understand your own feebleness and call for his help and cry loudly for him. The third reason is that you should never feel quite secure, for security begets carelessness and presumption and both these beget disobedience. The fourth reason why the Lord hides himself is that you may seek him more earnestly and call out and weep for him. And this is the fifth reason: that you should receive him the more gladly when he returns. And the sixth reason is that you should guard him more wisely and keep hold of him more firmly when you have caught him so that you may say with his beloved: I held him and I shall not let him go.

* CXXI *

GOD said to Margery Kempe in her vision: I act sometimes with my grace to you as I do with the sun. Sometimes, as you know well, the sun shines abroad so that many men may see it and sometimes it is hidden under a cloud so that men may not see it. Yet the sun is there nevertheless in his heat and his brightness and even so act I with you and my chosen souls.

* CXXII *

RICHARD ROLLE said: Sometimes the fiend tempts men and women that are solitary in a strange and subtle manner. He transfigures himself into the likeness of an angel of light and appears to them and says that he is one of God's angels come to comfort them and so he deceives fools. But they that are wise will not quickly trust to all spirits, but ask counsel of learned men he cannot beguile.

⋆ CXXIII ⋆

MARGERY KEMPE went to Dame Julian in Norwich and told her all her revelations from God so that she might know if there were any deceit in them, for the anchoress was an expert in such matters and could give good counsel. The anchoress, hearing the marvellous goodness of our Lord, greatly thanked God with all her heart for his visitation. She counselled Margery Kempe to be obedient to the will of our Lord God and to fulfil with all her might whatever he put in her soul if it were not against the worship of God and profit of her fellow Christians. If it was, then it was not the moving of a good spirit but rather of an evil spirit. The Holy Ghost never motivates anything against love and if he did he would be contrary to his own self for he is all love.

⋆ CXXIV ⋆

MARGERY KEMPE said: And sometimes, these things that men thought were revelations are deceits and illusions and therefore you ought not to give ready belief to every stirring but soberly to wait and pray as to whether it was sent from God.

AELRED wrote: Morality which engenders spiritual pride is not a virtue because pride itself, which is a vice, forces this which is considered a virtue into its own image and so it becomes not a virtue but a vice.

RICHARD ROLLE warned: Some the devil takes by making them think that the things that they do or say are best and for this reason they will accept no counsel from other men that are better and wiser than themselves. This is foul, stinking pride, for they esteem their wisdom greater than any others. Some the devil deceives through vainglory that is idle joy. They have pride and delight in themselves for the penance they have undergone, for the good deeds that they do, or for any virtue that they may have and are glad when men love them and sorry when men blame them and are envious of those of whom more good is spoken than of themselves. They hold themselves so glorious and so far above the life that other men lead, that they think no one should reprehend them in anything that they do or say and they despise sinful men and others that will not do as they bid them. How can you find a more sinful wretch than such a one? And what is much worse, he is held and honoured by men as wise and holy and does not know that he is evil. Some are deceived by overmuch greed and liking for meat and drink: they exceed due measure and come to excess and take delight therein. Some are beguiled with overmuch abstinence in meat and drink and sleep, which is the temptation of the devil for it causes them to fall in the midst of their work so that they do not bring it to completion as they would have done if they had shown wisdom and exercised discretion. So they lose their merit through their perversity.

* CXXVII *

IN *The Cloud* we read: Some men the fiend will deceive in this manner: in a wonderful way he will inflame their brains to maintain God's law and to destroy sin in all other men. He will never tempt them with a sin that is clearly evil. He makes them, like busy prelates, keep watch over all classes of Christian men alive, like an abbot superintending his monks. They will reprove all men's faults just as if they had spiritual charge of their souls and they think that they dare not act otherwise for fear of God. But they tell them all their faults that they see and they say that they have been stirred thereto by the fire of charity and of god's love in their hearts. But truly they lie, it is with the fire of hell welling up in their brains and their imagination.

* CXXVIII *

FATHER BAKER warned: Of all errors the greatest and most dangerous is the indiscreet imitation of the examples and practices of saints, in particular the extraordinary bodily mortification which they voluntarily (yet by God's special direction) assumed, such as labours, fastings, watchings, disciplines, etc. For such presumption in others, not called thereto, it is much to be feared, proceeds merely from pride and self-love and will produce no better effects than nourishing these vices. And above all things we must take heed that we do not entangle ourselves by laying obligations and vows upon our souls from which we shall have difficulty in disentangling ourselves when by trial we find them inconvenient.

* CXXIX *

THOMAS TRAHERNE wrote in his *Meditations*: Examine yourself well and you will find it a difficult matter to love God so as to die for him and not to love your brother so as to die for him in the same manner. Shall I not love him infinitely whom God loves infinitely and commends to my love as the representative of himself saying: What you do to him is done to me.

* CXXX *

WE READ in the *Ancrene Riwle*: Truly I believe that never shall the temptations of the flesh or of the spirit overmaster you if you are kind-hearted, humble and gentle and love so sincerely all men and women, that you are as sorry for their evil and glad of their good as for your own and wish that all who love you should love them as well as you and comfort them as well as you. If you have a knife or garment, food or drink, scroll or book, a holy man's comfort or any other thing that would benefit them, choose to go without it yourself so that they might have it.

WALTER HILTON wrote: Our Lord has sent into your heart a little sparkle of this blessed fire; that is himself. As the holy writ says: Our God is a consuming fire. For as bodily fire consumes all bodily things that can be consumed, even so spiritual fire, that is God, consumes all manner of sins wheresoever it falls; therefore our Lord is likened to a consuming fire. I pray you nourish this fire which is nothing else but love and charity. God has sent the fire of his Love—a good desire and great will to please him—into a man's soul to this end: that man should know it, keep it, nourish it and strengthen it and be saved thereby. The more desire that you have for him the more is this fire of love in you; the less your desire is the less is this fire. The measure of this desire in yourself and in any other person you do not know, nor does any man himself know, but only God who gives it. And therefore do not dispute with yourself as if you would know how much your desire is, but strive to desire as much as you can and not that you may know the measure of your desire.

THOMAS TRAHERNE wrote: By this love we become heirs of all men's joys, and coheirs with Christ. For what is the reason of your own joys when you are blessed with good things? Is it not self-love? If you loved others as you love yourself, you would be as much affected with their joys. If you loved them more, more. For according to the measure of your love to others will you be happy in them, for according to it you will be delightful to them and delighted in your happiness. The more you love men, the more delightful you will be to God, and the more delight you will take in God, and the more you will enjoy him. So that the more like you are to him in goodness, the more abundantly you will enjoy his goodness. By loving others you will live in others to receive it.

* CXXXIII *

IN THE *Ancrene Riwle* we read: As I have said, the remedy for envy is brotherly love and doing good and goodwill where the power to act is wanting. So much strength have love and goodwill that in their working they make another's good, our good as well. Only love his good and be well pleased and glad of it and so you turn it to you and make it your own. St Gregory bears witness to it: If you delight in another's good you make it your own. If you envy another's good you poison yourself with a healing draught and wound yourself with ointment.

* CXXXIV *

JULIAN OF NORWICH said: A glad giver takes little heed of the thing that he gives, but his desire and his purpose is to please him and comfort him to whom he gives it. If the receiver takes the gift with appreciation and thankfully then the courteous giver counts for nothing all his cost and all his toil for joy and delight that he has pleased and comforted him that he loves.

⋆ CXXXV ⋆

MARGERY KEMPE prayed many times and often in these words: Lord for thy great goodness have mercy on all my wickedness as certainly I was never as wicked as you are good nor ever may be though I would. For you are so good that you cannot be better and therefore it is a great wonder that ever any man should be parted from you for ever.

⋆ CXXXVI ⋆

WILLIAM LAW says of hell: Hell is nothing else but nature departed or excluded from the beams of divine light.

⋆ CXXXVII ⋆

JOHN SMITH said: Hell is rather a nature than a place and heaven cannot be so truly defined by anything without us as something that is within us.

⋆ CXXXVIII ⋆

THOMAS TRAHERNE added: They in heaven prize blessings when they have them. They on earth do not prize them when they have them. They in hell prize them but do not have them.

⋆ CXXXIX ⋆

J. W. ROWNTREE wrote: Sin carries its own bitter punishment with it. Lust breeds satiety and loathing and selfishness breeds a morose sour spirit joyless as a subterranean cavern. Hell is separation from God and the longer we live in hell the harder it is to escape. Character congeals; as it grows it stiffens and takes shape, ugly or beautiful according to our absence from God or his presence with us.

WILLIAM LAW says in an address to the clergy: If long, long ages of fiery pain and tormenting darkness fall to the share of many or most of God's fallen creatures, they will last no longer than that time when the great fire of God has melted all arrogance into humility and all that is self has died in the long agonies and bloody sweat of a lost God, which is that all-saving cross of Christ which will never give up its redeeming power till all sin and sinners have no more name among the creatures of God.

RICHARD ROLLE wrote: There is no one more blessed than he who can die because of the greatness of his love. No creature can love too much. In all other things that which is done in excess turns to vice but the virtue of love is that the more it abounds the more glorious it will be.

AELRED WROTE: What, I ask, can be more sweet, what more peaceful, than not to be stirred up by the strong motions of the flesh, not to be burnt by the fires of carnal desires, not to be drawn to any seductive apparition? To have the flesh cooled by the dew of chastity, subservient to the spirit, not enticed by the carnal pleasures but a most obedient helper in spiritual exercises? What can approach so nearly to divine tranquillity as to be moved by no insults heaped upon us, to fear no punishment or persecution, to have the same constancy of mind in prosperity and adversity, to look with the same eyes on foe and friend and to conform oneself into the likeness of him who makes his sun to rise over the good and evil, and rain to fall on the just and unjust. All these things exist in love and nowhere else except in love and thence in it is true tranquillity, true pleasure because it is the yoke of the Lord and if by his invitation we bear it we find rest for our souls for the yoke of the Lord is pleasant and his burden light.

★ CXLIII ★

WE READ in *The Cloud*: God regards with his merciful eyes not what you are nor what you have been but what you wish to be.

★ CXLIV ★

RUPERT BROOKE, the soldier poet, wrote:

We have built a house that is not for Times throwing
We have gained a peace unshaken by pain for ever.
War knows no power. Safe shall be my going,
Secretly armed against all death's endeavour;
Safe though all safety's lost; safe where men fall;
And if these poor limbs die, safest of all.

JOHN MASEFIELD, the poet laureate, wrote of Sir Bors:

Would I could win some quiet and rest, and a little
  ease,
In the cool grey hush of the dusk, in the dim green
  place of the trees,
Where the birds are singing, singing, singing, crying
  aloud
The song of the red, red rose that blossoms beyond the
  seas.

Would I could see it, the rose, when the light begins to
  fail
And the lone white star in the West is glimmering on
  the mail;
The red, red passionate rose of the sacred blood of
  Christ,
In the shining chalice of God, the cup of the Holy
  Grail.

It will happen at last, at dusk, as my horse limps down
  the fell,
A star will glow like a note God strikes on a silver bell,
And the bright white birds of God will carry my soul
  to Christ,
And the sight of the Rose, the Rose, will pay for the
  years of hell.

★ CXLVI ★

WILLIAM BLAKE wrote in the *Book of 'Thel'*:

And all shall say, 'Without a use this shining woman
  liv'd,

Or did she only live to be at death the food of worms?'
The Cloud reclined upon his airy throne and answered
    thus;
'Then if thou art the food of worms, O virgin of the
    skies,
How great thy use, how great thy blessing! Everything
    that lives
Lives not alone nor for itself.'

★ CXLVII ★

BETWEEN the business of life and the day of death a space ought to be interposed.

★ CXLVIII ★

FATHER BAKER wrote: It is not without just reason that an ancient holy man said that a religious spiritual life is a continual meditation of death because the principal end of all our exercises is to prepare ourselves against the day of our great account, to the end we may give it with joy and not with fear.

★ CXLIX ★

MARY COLERIDGE, the poetess, wrote:

> Sunshine let it be or frost
> Storm or calm, as Thou shalt choose;
> Though Thine every gift were lost,
> Thee Thyself we could not lose.